Prayers
FOR MY
Baby Girl

KATIE KENNY PHILLIPS
ILLUSTRATED BY AUDREY JEANNE ROBERTS

HARVEST HOUSE PUBLISHERS
EUGENE, OREGON

Katie Kenny Phillips

is the author of several children's books, including *Today I Feel Like a Jelly Donut*; *God, You Make Me Feel Special*; *Jesus Loves Everybody*; and *Let's Find Joy!* with Shaunti Feldhahn. Katie lives in Atlanta, Georgia, with her husband, five kids, and their ridiculous dogs, Norm and Coco.

Unless otherwise noted, all Scripture verses are taken from the *Holy Bible*, New Living Translation, copyright © 1996, 2004, 2015 by Tyndale House Foundation. Used with permission of Tyndale House Publishers, Carol Stream, Illinois 60188. All rights reserved.

Verses marked ESV are taken from the ESV® Bible (The Holy Bible, English Standard Version®), copyright © 2001 by Crossway, a publishing ministry of Good News Publishers. Used with permission. All rights reserved. The ESV text may not be quoted in any publication made available to the public by a Creative Commons license. The ESV may not be translated in whole or in part into any other language.

Cover and interior design by Nicole Dougherty

This logo is a federally registered trademark of the Hawkins Children's LLC. Harvest House Publishers, Inc., is the exclusive licensee of this trademark.

Prayers for My Baby Girl

Text copyright © 2025 by Harvest House Publishers
Artwork copyright © 2025 by Audrey Jeanne Roberts, courtesy of MHS Licensing
Published by Harvest House Publishers
Eugene, Oregon 97408
www.harvesthousepublishers.com

ISBN 978-0-7369-9217-6 (hardcover)

Library of Congress Control Number: 2025937792

No part of this book may be used or reproduced in any manner for the purpose of training artificial intelligence technologies or systems.

All rights reserved. No part of this publication may be reproduced, stored in a retrieval system, or transmitted in any form or by any means—electronic, mechanical, digital, photocopy, recording, or any other—except for brief quotations in printed reviews, without the prior permission of the publisher.

Printed in China

25 26 27 28 29 30 31 32 33 / DC / 10 9 8 7 6 5 4 3 2 1

Everyone must submit to governing authorities. For all authority comes from God, and those in positions of authority have been placed there by God.

ROMANS 13:1

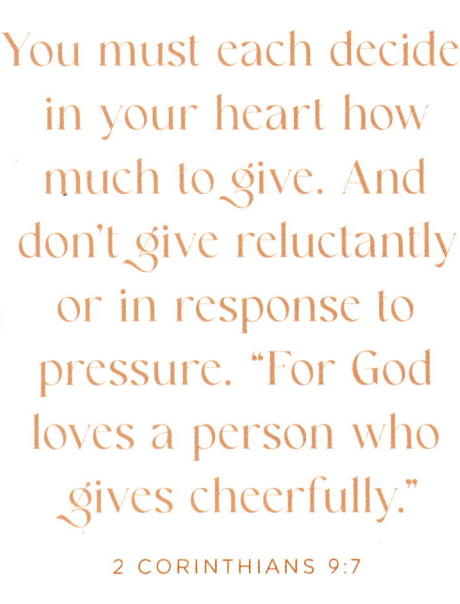

You must each decide in your heart how much to give. And don't give reluctantly or in response to pressure. "For God loves a person who gives cheerfully."

2 CORINTHIANS 9:7

HEALTHY BOUNDARIES

Dear God,

I ask that You'd instill healthy boundaries and a clear understanding of when to say yes and when to say no, according to Your will. Help her resist peer pressure, and give her a cheerful heart when she decides to give and a settled heart and mind when she doesn't (2 Corinthians 9:7). Whatever she seeks to do, remind her to pray for wisdom in all things, and help her hear Your strong, clear voice for direction.

Amen.

BLESSING

Dear God,

I don't know the plans You have for this sweet child, but I know she is destined to be a blessing. To me, to others, and to You. Thank You for promising Your Holy Spirit to her when she accepts You as her Savior, and I ask that once she does, You would propel her into the world as a blessing wherever You lead her (Acts 1:8). Allow her testimony to impact every person she meets.

Amen.

You will receive power when the Holy Spirit comes upon you. And you will be my witnesses, telling people about me everywhere—in Jerusalem, throughout Judea, in Samaria, and to the ends of the earth.

ACTS 1:8

[God] will once again fill your mouth with laughter and your lips with shouts of joy.

JOB 8:21

DELIGHT

Dear God,

Bless this girl with a lifetime of laughter and delight. Give her a spirit of joy, as a blessing not only to herself but to everyone around her. Have her lips be quick with a smile, a praise, a song, and uplifting words (Job 8:21) that will make others flock to her and her positivity. Allow her to be diligent in seeking out the good rather than focusing on the negative. Help her lead the way as others curiously follow her journey toward joy.

                                              Amen.

JUSTICE

Father God,

Compel this baby girl to always do what is right in Your eyes, regardless of what others say or do. May her actions always show mercy so others can see the Holy Spirit at work within her and draw them closer to You (Micah 6:8). I ask that she humbly walk with You so she can be an effective advocate for justice for the most vulnerable among us. Use her to make the world a better, more compassionate place.

Amen.

O people, the Lord has told you what is good, and this is what he requires of you: to do what is right, to love mercy, and to walk humbly with your God.

MICAH 6:8

When you are praying,
first forgive anyone you
are holding a grudge against,
so that your Father in heaven
will forgive your sins, too.

MARK 11:25

FORGIVENESS

Forgiving Father,

I'm so thankful for Your forgiveness, and I know You sent Your Son to die on the cross for our sins. I ask that this baby girl learn the magnitude of Your gift at an early age and recognize the importance of forgiveness. As she learns this, please give her a compassionate heart that forgives others quickly and completely, knowing You require us to forgive others (Mark 11:25). Help me model this for her, and as she grows, may she become a beautiful example of Your sacrificial love for us.

Amen.

PERSEVERANCE

Dear God,

Give this child endurance for the race ahead. Throughout her beautiful, complicated, wonderful, challenging life, she needs to learn the lessons of endurance so she may become a woman of strong character who has the confident hope of salvation in You (Romans 5:3-5). Surround her with mentors who encourage her to challenge herself. To push herself. To rely more on You than she does on herself. Help her endure this life training, appreciate the journey, and arrive strong at the finish line with salvation as her ultimate prize.

Amen.

We can rejoice, too, when we run into problems and trials, for we know that they help us develop endurance. And endurance develops strength of character, and character strengthens our confident hope of salvation. And this hope will not lead to disappointment. For we know how dearly God loves us, because he has given us the Holy Spirit to fill our hearts with his love.

ROMANS 5:3-5

We are careful to be honorable before the Lord, but we also want everyone else to see that we are honorable.

2 CORINTHIANS 8:21

HONESTY

Dear God,

Wrap honesty and integrity around this baby girl like a cloak. Allow these to be a source of warmth and strength throughout her life. Will You give her the desire to always speak the truth, no matter how difficult it might be? I know You want us to be honest not only when we pray to You but also in our everyday thoughts, words, and actions (2 Corinthians 8:21). Make her lips speak truth with love, and may her life be a living testimony as others watch and see Your goodness.

Amen.

COMPASSION

Comforting Father,

How grateful I am to know You will comfort this child throughout her life. While I wish my child would never be troubled, I am thankful Your love and tenderness will allow her to learn how to comfort others—and she will be a blessing to those in similar circumstances (2 Corinthians 1:3-4). Help her to have a heart for those who need Your compassion, including herself. When it comes to generosity, may she be overflowing with compassion to others in need.

Amen.

All praise to God, the Father of our Lord Jesus Christ. God is our merciful Father and the source of all comfort. He comforts us in all our troubles so that we can comfort others. When they are troubled, we will be able to give them the same comfort God has given us.

2 CORINTHIANS 1:3-4

"I know the plans I have for you," says the Lord. "They are plans for good and not for disaster, to give you a future and a hope."

JEREMIAH 29:11

FRUITFULNESS

Heavenly Father,

Give this child a long and fruitful life, a scrapbook filled with rewarding relationships, meaningful work, and countless miracles that reveal Your loving-kindness. Light the path before her, even if it's just a few steps at a time, as she follows You in faith. Though her future is unknown, I trust this baby girl to You because You promise Your plans for her are good and hopeful (Jeremiah 29:11). Be close to her as her Savior, companion, and protector, and guide her through every page of her life story.

Amen.

DESIRE TO BE LIKE JESUS

Dear God,

There will be so many people this baby girl admires throughout her life, and I hope I am one of them. But above all else, I want her to look up to You so she can imitate the best example of all. Give this child the desire to imitate Jesus and to love others because everyone is Your image bearer (Ephesians 5:1). By caring for others as You do, she will be a walking, talking messenger of Your love throughout the world. Help her see people and circumstances and the world with Your compassionate, loving eyes. May her heart beat in rhythm with Yours.

Amen.

Imitate God, therefore, in everything you do, because you are his dear children.

EPHESIANS 5:1

Don't worry about anything; instead, pray about everything. Tell God what you need, and thank him for all he has done. Then you will experience God's peace, which exceeds anything we can understand. His peace will guard your hearts and minds as you live in Christ Jesus.

PHILIPPIANS 4:6-7

PRAYER LIFE

Dear Heavenly Father,

I ask You to bless this girl's prayer life. Through all her days, call her to an ongoing, intimate, and meaningful conversation with You. Create a thread between Your heart and hers, so she may feel the pull to be close to You. As she grows, tap her on the shoulder, whisper in her ear, sing to her. You promise if she comes to You in prayer and thanksgiving, Your peace will guard her heart and mind (Philippians 4:6-7). Lord, may Your voice be the one she always longs to hear.

Amen.

DISCERNMENT

Dear God,

In a world that will constantly try to pull this child away from You, I ask that You give my daughter discernment so she can always hear Your good and perfect will. Sound alarms in her spirit to help her resist the temptations that are harmful, and illuminate the path of righteousness. Make her into a new creation, giving her clarity of mind, focus, and the desire to live a transformed life each and every day (Romans 12:2).

Amen.

Don't copy the behavior and customs of this world, but let God transform you into a new person by changing the way you think. Then you will learn to know God's will for you, which is good and pleasing and perfect.

ROMANS 12:2

We are his workmanship, created in Christ Jesus for good works, which God prepared beforehand, that we should walk in them.

EPHESIANS 2:10 ESV

CREATIVITY

Dear God,

What wonderful things You have planned for this child throughout her life! Use her mind and hands and feet and creativity to bless the world with good works (Ephesians 2:10). Allow her eyes to see beyond the ordinary, ears to hear goodness, a mouth that praises, feet that serve, and an imagination open wide to everything You have in store for her. May her life leave a mark on humanity that reveals Your character and love.

Amen.

UNIQUENESS

Dear God,

I know too well that this precious baby girl was formed with precision by Your loving hand. You created her in Your image and love her exactly the way she's designed. Give her the soul-deep knowledge that she is worthy because she is fearfully and wonderfully made and Your work is always good (Psalm 139:14). Help her appreciate her uniqueness as a gift from You and use that knowledge to live a life of purpose to lead others to You.

Amen.

I praise you, for I am fearfully
and wonderfully made.
Wonderful are your works;
my soul knows it very well.

PSALM 139:14 ESV

We can make our plans, but the Lord determines our steps.

PROVERBS 16:9

FUTURE

Good Father,

I have dreams for this child, ones that include happiness and contentment with a family of her own one day. If that is Your will for her, Lord, please prepare a husband for her who is loving, kind, patient, compassionate, and, above all, a Jesus follower. If it is not Your plan for her to marry or have children, prepare for her a rich and wonderful life, filled to the brim with love and community. Whatever is in store for this child, prepare her heart to be loving and loved (Proverbs 16:9).

Amen.

DETERMINATION

Dear God,

I want to believe that this little girl's life will be easy, but I know it will not always be so. Give her moments—even in the midst of struggle and discomfort and stretching and growth—where she is determined to strain forward to what lies ahead and seek the prize of whatever or wherever You call her (Philippians 3:12-14). Help her dig deep and find Your strength there, knowing that pushing forward into Your will is the safest and surest direction she can travel.

Amen.

Not that I have already obtained this or am already perfect, but I press on to make it my own, because Christ Jesus has made me his own...One thing I do: forgetting what lies behind and straining forward to what lies ahead, I press on toward the goal for the prize of the upward call of God in Christ Jesus.

PHILIPPIANS 3:12-14 ESV

We know that God causes everything to work together for the good of those who love God and are called according to his purpose for them.

ROMANS 8:28

PURPOSE

Lord God,

Please give this child a full and beautiful life. Give her a sense of calling that aligns with Your will. You have plans for her that are good, and You promise to work things together for Your purposes (Romans 8:28). Help her lean into Your vision for her future and measure success by Your standards. When the world tries to sway her into striving and focusing on herself, keep her eyes steady on You and Your greater story. Make her life's purpose reflect Your glory.

Amen.

Work willingly at whatever you do, as though you were working for the Lord rather than for people.

COLOSSIANS 3:23

WORK ETHIC

Dear God,

I ask that You give this child the desire to work hard and willingly at whatever she does and to commit her work to You (Colossians 3:23). In a world that values shortcuts and quick fixes, may she do what needs to be done to the best of her ability—especially when no one is looking. Let her feel the satisfaction of a job well done and inspire others with her commitment to integrity and excellence. Whatever she chooses to do—from her daily tasks to opportunities to serve others to her future occupation—let her actions always be a sweet, fragrant offering to You.

Amen.

GRATITUDE

Gracious God,

Give this little girl the desire to plant seeds of gratitude along the winding pathway of her life. Her moments will be filled with ups and downs, good and bad, the easy and the difficult, but with Your help she can trust You and give You thanks for each circumstance (1 Thessalonians 5:18). As she matures, I pray she sees a bountiful harvest of blessings, proving that belonging to Jesus results in a fruitful and heart-filled life.

Amen.

Be thankful in all circumstances, for this is God's will for you who belong to Christ Jesus.

1 THESSALONIANS 5:18

Since we are receiving a Kingdom that is unshakable, let us be thankful and please God by worshiping him with holy fear and awe.

HEBREWS 12:28

WONDER

Wonderful God,

What a glorious thing for this baby girl to discover that she can inherit an unshakeable kingdom from You! Give her lips to express gratitude for this gift, and a posture of gratitude as she learns more and more about worshiping an awesome and holy God (Hebrews 12:28). May she never lose her sense of wonder at who You are and what You've done for her. Color her world in such a way that she cannot deny Your artist touch.

Amen.

CURIOSITY

Dear God,

This is the day You have made, and I thank You for the reminder that we can always rejoice and be glad in it (Psalm 118:24)! Give this baby girl the desire to seek out joy in the midst of hardship, gratitude in the midst of the mundane, and blessings in the midst of the ordinary. Will You allow her to be curious enough to see Your goodness every day, regardless of her circumstances? Help her fight the culture of negativity and be a noticer of all Your praiseworthy things.

Amen.

This is the day the Lord has made. We will rejoice and be glad in it.

PSALM 118:24

This is my command—be strong and courageous! Do not be afraid or discouraged. For the Lord your God is with you wherever you go.

JOSHUA 1:9

COURAGE

Father,

If I could protect this baby girl from being swallowed up by fear throughout her life, I would do it. But I know I cannot. There will be plenty of moments when I won't be there and she will need Your supernatural courage and presence. Go everywhere with her, Lord. Stick so close that she can feel You beside her. You promise she can be strong and courageous, not fearful or discouraged, because You are always with her (Joshua 1:9). Help her never, ever doubt Your promised presence.

Amen.

SELF-CONTROL

Dear God,

There are so many amazing opportunities and experiences ahead for this child. So many people to meet, places to travel, things to learn, and ideas to explore. Will You give her the wisdom and self-control to go forth into this world without fear but with Your power and love (2 Timothy 1:7)? Help her know each step she should take and what she should avoid, and allow her to trust in the communication You will share. Be clear in Your instructions to her, and in that clarity, her self-control will grow stronger every day.

Amen.

God has not given us
a spirit of fear and
timidity, but of power,
love, and self-discipline.

2 TIMOTHY 1:7

Always be humble and gentle. Be patient with each other, making allowance for each other's faults because of your love.

EPHESIANS 4:2

GENTLENESS

Gentle Father,

As I hold this child and gently rock her, I know full well You are holding her in Your arms as well. Give her a spirit of gentleness with others, allowing people to feel cared for and understood whenever they are in her presence. Make people stop in wonder at her kindness, and when they spend time with her, give them a sense of Your life-light burning quietly and humbly inside her (Ephesians 4:2).

Amen.

FAITHFULNESS

Good Father,

I ask that You draw this baby girl into Yourself from her earliest days and make her heart beat for You. When life becomes challenging, please give her the steadfastness and faithfulness to trust in Jesus, even on days and on paths that seem difficult. While she cannot see You, may she feel You beside her as if You are holding her hand (Hebrews 11:1). As the two of you walk together, Your presence will increase and bolster her faith on whatever journey You are guiding her along.

Amen.

Faith shows the reality of what we hope for; it is the evidence of things we cannot see.

HEBREWS 11:1

Let's not get tired of doing what is good. At just the right time we will reap a harvest of blessing if we don't give up.

GALATIANS 6:9

PATIENCE

Holy God,

You designed this precious baby girl, and her future is full of opportunities to reveal Your glory to others through her actions, words, and prayers. Allow her to hear Your voice when You call her and to work with endurance, and give her the strength to not grow tired of doing good, as it will reap blessings (Galatians 6:9). Help her see the value in planting seeds, watering them, and harvesting based on Your will—and to be patient enough to wait on Your perfect timing.

Amen.

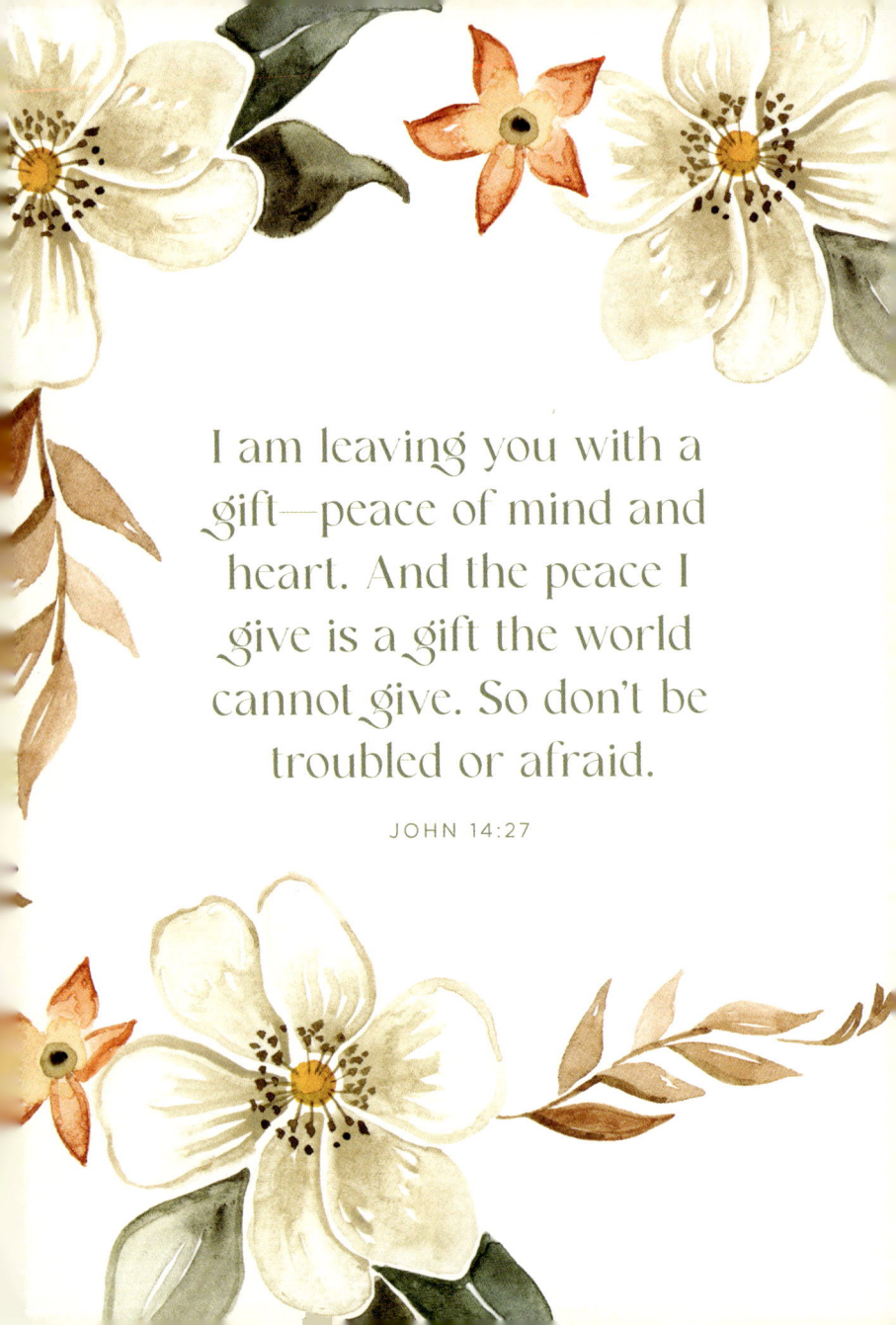

I am leaving you with a gift—peace of mind and heart. And the peace I give is a gift the world cannot give. So don't be troubled or afraid.

JOHN 14:27

PEACE

Dear God,

You are the giver of good, good gifts, and I praise You for the gift of Your peace. Bless this baby girl with peace of mind and heart—not as the world gives but as only You can (John 14:27). There will be many moments throughout her life that will feel uncertain, but I ask You to pour out Your peace as if anointing her with oil, covering her and marking her as Your own.

Amen.

JOY

Good Father,

Thank You for the blessing of this baby girl. Please give her eyes to see You, a heart to trust You, and a glorious, inexpressible joy (1 Peter 1:8-9) because You call her Yours. Allow this child to live her life with such overflowing, tangible joy that anyone who comes into contact with her cannot deny You are the source of all that is worthy to be praised.

Amen.

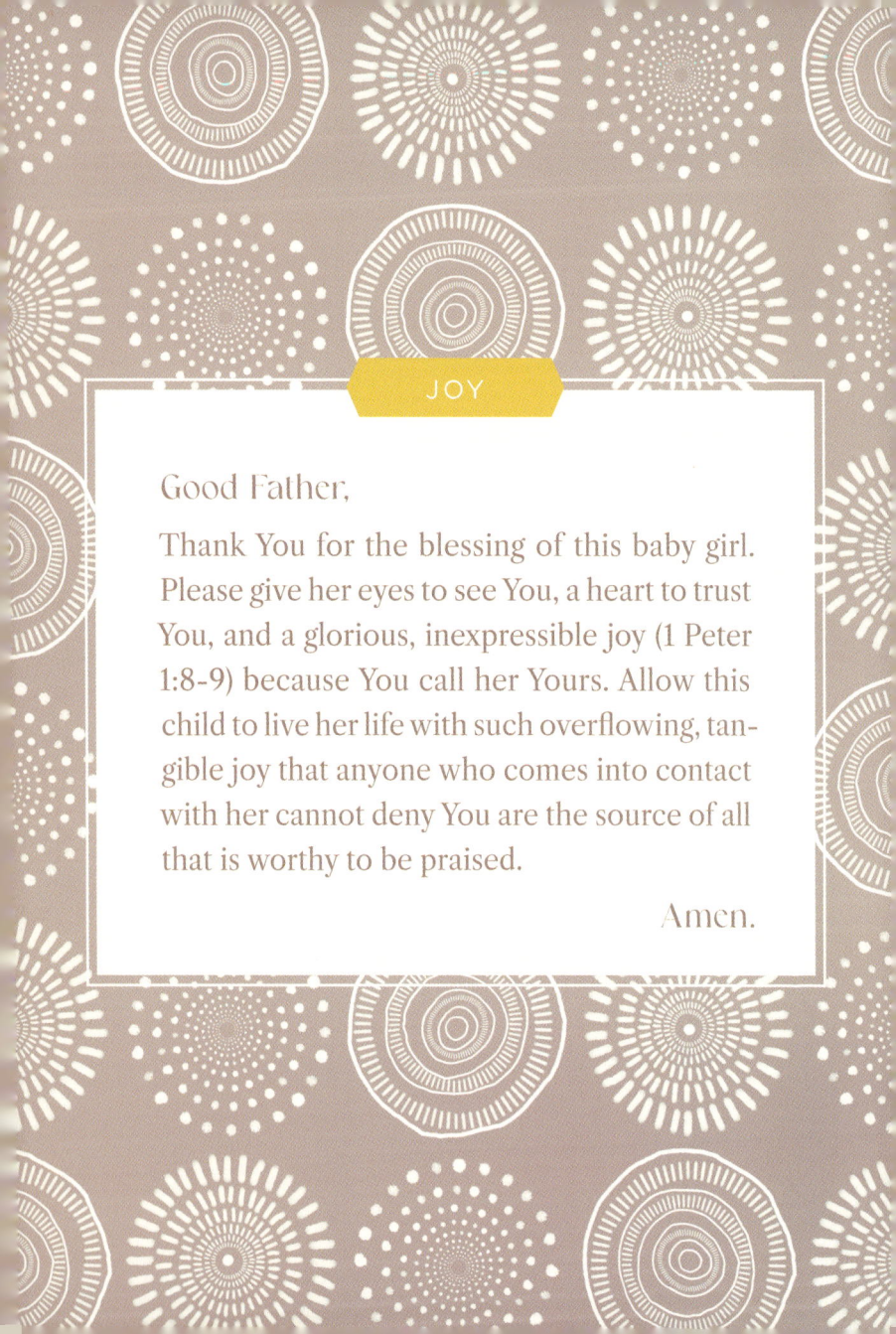

You love [God] even though you have never seen him. Though you do not see him now, you trust him; and you rejoice with a glorious, inexpressible joy. The reward for trusting him will be the salvation of your souls.

1 PETER 1:8-9

God decided in advance to adopt us into his own family by bringing us to himself through Jesus Christ. This is what he wanted to do, and it gave him great pleasure.

EPHESIANS 1:5

VALUE

Loving God,

I have longed for this child, and she is a blessing. Thank You for bringing her into our family—a treasure more valuable than I could have imagined. Please help her know how much she is loved every day of her life—by us, of course, but also by You, her Heavenly Father. May she know deep in her bones that she was adopted into Your family through Jesus Christ and that her existence was created with intention, precision, purpose, and great pleasure (Ephesians 1:5).

Amen.

KINDNESS

Kind Father,

Thank You for making this baby girl in Your likeness. I ask that this child radiate Your goodness to the world around her, revealing Your character and drawing people to You. May this sweet soul be kind and tenderhearted to everyone she meets, always remembering to forgive others as You have forgiven us (Ephesians 4:32). When she does this, she will always be an arrow pointing directly to You.

Amen.

Be kind to each other, tenderhearted, forgiving one another, just as God through Christ has forgiven you.

EPHESIANS 4:32

Whatever you give
is acceptable if you give it
eagerly. And give according
to what you have, not
what you don't have.

2 CORINTHIANS 8:12

GENEROSITY

Generous Father,

I pray a spirit of generosity over my daughter. Give her a soft and compassionate heart to serve others. Open her eyes to those around her. Be a clear and steady voice in her ear so she can hear Your call. Use her life as a way to show others Your goodness, kindness, and mercy. Your Word says that You accept the gifts of Your children, both big and small, when the willingness is there (2 Corinthians 8:12). May her generosity and service be an acceptable gift when she loves others as You do.

Amen.

EDUCATION

Dear God,

Thank You for the mind inside this precious baby's head. Give her the desire and the drive to seek knowledge and wisdom throughout her life. Allow her education—both in school and in life—to propel her toward the good works You have created for her to do. Give her ears that are open to learning new things (Proverbs 18:15), and bless her with a deep curiosity about people, places, cultures, and experiences so she can live an honorable, well-rounded life in this incredible world You've created.

Amen.

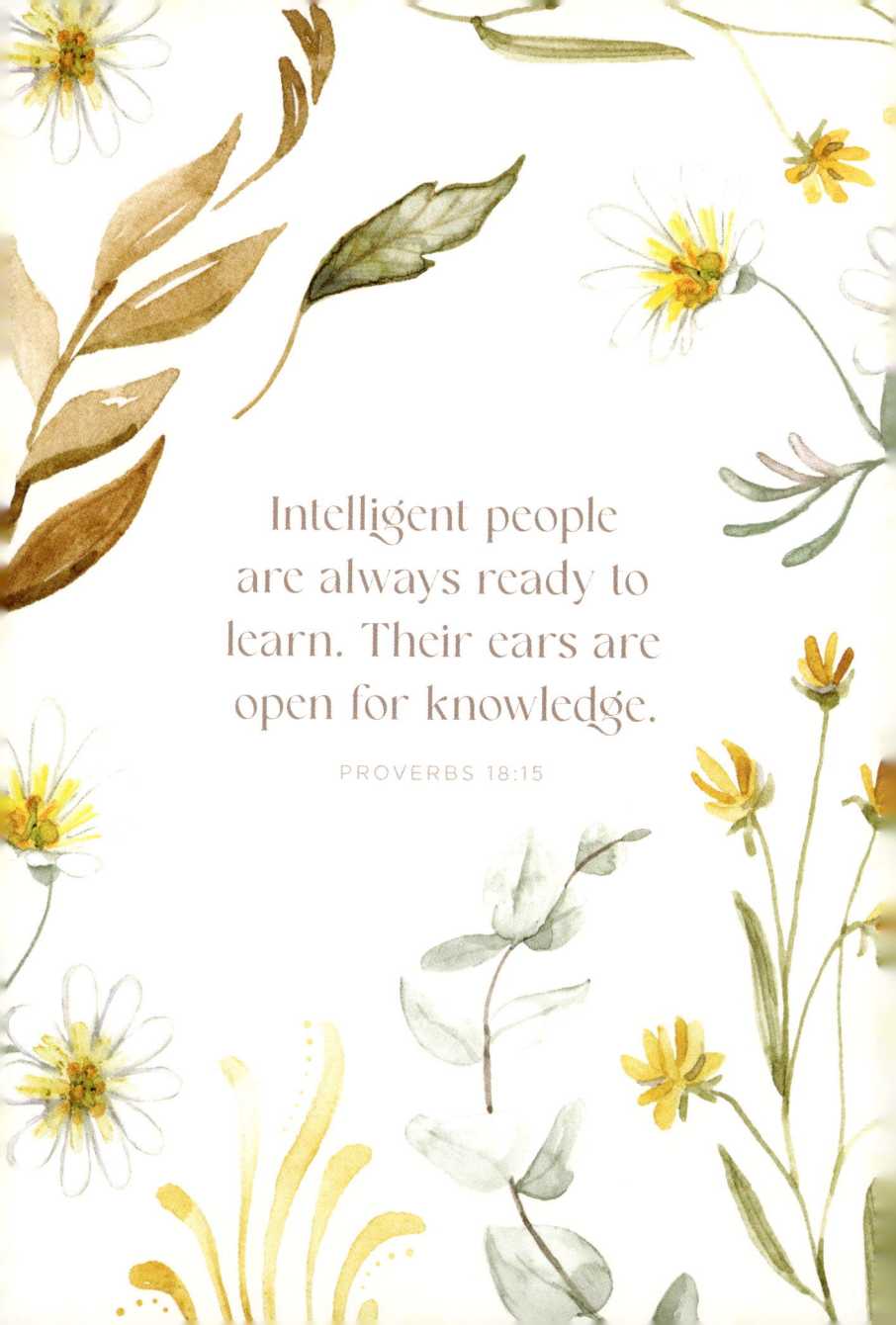

Intelligent people are always ready to learn. Their ears are open for knowledge.

PROVERBS 18:15

Let us think of ways to motivate one another to acts of love and good works. And let us not neglect our meeting together, as some people do, but encourage one another, especially now that the day of his return is drawing near.

HEBREWS 10:24-25

COMMUNITY

Dear Father,

Thank You for the community You've prepared for this baby girl throughout her life. I trust You to gather together believers who will love her and be a source of encouragement and strength as she seeks to follow You in this big, beautiful world (Hebrews 10:24-25). May she also have a heart for Your people—serving, comforting, and supporting others as they do the same for her. Make these relationships rich and meaningful—reminders that our relationships are some of Your very best gifts.

Amen.

SIBLINGS

Dear God,

Bless this baby girl in her relationships with her siblings—both now and in the future. Whether they are within our family or she considers others as close as a sister or brother, grow this baby's heart to bursting with compassion, love, and kindness. Give her the opportunity to not only be loyal but present—noticing, seeing—and a true source of help for her siblings when she is needed most (Proverbs 17:17).

Amen.

A friend is always loyal, and a brother is born to help in time of need.

PROVERBS 17:17

Children are a gift from the Lord; they are a reward from him.

PSALM 127:3

OUR RELATIONSHIP

Dear Heavenly Father,

This baby girl is an incredible gift and reward from You (Psalm 127:3), and I thank You for allowing me the opportunity to pour into her life. Help me to live with intention and to invest in both small and big moments throughout her lifetime. Foster between us a loving, trusting, healthy relationship that not only brings us joy and blessings but also glorifies You and brings You honor.

Amen.

RELATIONSHIP WITH JESUS

Dear God,

Thank You for sending Your Son to save my precious daughter. Guide her daily along the illuminated path toward Jesus—the way, the truth, and the life (John 14:6)—offering her the promise of eternal unity with You. I ask that when Your timing is right, You would allow her to accept Jesus as her personal Savior and walk the rest of her days in relationship with Him.

Amen.

Jesus told him, "I am the way, the truth, and the life. No one can come to the Father except through me."

JOHN 14:6

Do not be afraid or discouraged, for the Lord will personally go ahead of you. He will be with you; he will neither fail you nor abandon you.

DEUTERONOMY 31:8

PROTECTION

Heavenly Father,

I lay this beautiful child at Your feet. I love her more than I could ever fathom, and it humbles me to know You love her even more. I also lay down my fear and anxiety over her safety and ask You to protect her all the days of her life. I know she does not need to be afraid because You go before her, walk beside her, and will never fail her or abandon her (Deuteronomy 31:8). Help her to always feel Your presence, even when she is alone. And help me loosen my grip as I trust in Your love and care for her.

Amen.

WISDOM

Gracious Father,

Give this child a desire for wisdom that only You can supply. Let her seek it as if it were treasure—precious and valuable and life-giving. You tell us that when we need wisdom, we can ask You and You will not withhold it (James 1:5). Thank You for promising to give her the answers she needs and for instilling this yearning for Your will within her heart.

Amen.

> If you need wisdom, ask our generous God, and he will give it to you. He will not rebuke you for asking.
>
> JAMES 1:5